DATE DUE

EDGE BOOKS™

SPIES

[COLD WAR] SPIES

by TIM O'SHEI

Consultant:
Jan Goldman, EdD
Founding Board Member
International Intelligence Ethics Association
Washington, D.C.

Capstone press®

Mankato, Minnesota

Edge Books are published by Capstone Press,
151 Good Counsel Drive, P.O. Box 669, Mankato, Minnesota 56002.
www.capstonepress.com

Library of Congress Cataloging-in-Publication Data
O'Shei, Tim.
    Cold War spies / by Tim O'Shei.
    p. cm. — (Edge books. Spies)
    Summary: "Discusses the history of spying during the Cold War" —
Provided by publisher.
    Includes bibliographical references and index.
    ISBN-13: 978-1-4296-1305-7 (hardcover)
    ISBN-10: 1-4296-1305-X (hardcover)
    1. Cold War — Juvenile literature. 2. Espionage — History — 20th
century — Juvenile literature. I. Title. II. Series.
D843.O68 2008
327.1209'045 — dc22   2007033575

Editorial Credits

Angie Kaelberer, editor; Bob Lentz, designer; Jo Miller, photo researcher

Photo Credits

Alamy/Popperfoto, 27
AP Images, cover, 19 (bottom), 23, 24; Edwin Reichert, 21; Joint Task Force One, 12;
    Marty Lederhandler, 7
Corbis/Bettmann, 15, 16, 19 (top)
Getty Images Inc./Imagno/Hulton Archive, 10; Keystone/Hulton Archive, 8; Time Life
    Pictures/Dirck Halstead, 29
John F. Kennedy Library/National Park Service/Abbie Rowe, 4
Shutterstock/Aga, 1; Feng Yu, 9

1 2 3 4 5 6 13 12 11 10 09 08

[TABLE of CONTENTS]

CHAPTER 1

CRISIS IN CUBA

LEARN ABOUT:
The need for information
Another type of war
Missiles in Cuba

> President John F. Kennedy was elected in 1960 and served until November 1963.

The U.S. president's job is to lead the country and protect the American people. But the president can't do it alone. In October 1962, the United States faced the threat of nuclear war. President John F. Kennedy needed help. He needed information. He needed spies.

POWER STRUGGLE

For years, the United States and the Soviet Union had been in a power struggle. This situation was known as the Cold War. It wasn't a war fought on a battlefield. Instead, each country raced to build bigger armies, create deadlier weapons, and gain more power.

The United States and the Soviet Union didn't get along. But each had friends around the world. These countries were known as allies. The island country of Cuba was a Soviet ally.

In 1962, the news that the Soviets had sent nuclear missiles to Cuba alarmed Americans. Cuba is only 90 miles (145 kilometers) off the coast of Florida. Missiles there could reach the United States within minutes of launch.

Kennedy had to convince the Soviets to get the missiles out of Cuba. But it wasn't easy. Kennedy had to make a deal with the Soviets. To do that, he needed as much information as he could get.

Enter the American spies.

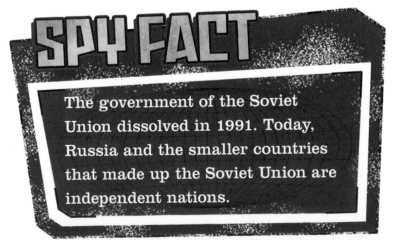

SPY FACT

The government of the Soviet Union dissolved in 1991. Today, Russia and the smaller countries that made up the Soviet Union are independent nations.

> Cuban leader Fidel Castro (left) and Soviet leader Nikita Khrushchev (right) were close allies.

CHAPTER 2

A WAR OF DISTRUST

LEARN ABOUT:
East and West
Iron Curtain
Spy agencies

> During World War II, British Prime Minister Winston Churchill (left), U.S. President Harry Truman (center), and Soviet Premier Joseph Stalin (right) worked together to defeat Germany.

The Cold War began shortly after the end of World War II (1939–1945). The United States and the Soviet Union were allies during World War II. Even so, neither country trusted the other. They were very different.

The Soviet Union was a **communist** country. The government provided people's jobs, homes, and the money they earned. But the government also chose the leaders and limited people's individual rights. The United States is a democracy. Its people can own their homes and choose their jobs and government leaders.

Both the Americans and the Soviets wanted to keep developing nuclear weapons. Both wished to be the first to send people into space. Both countries wanted the strongest military. Both stood ready to defend themselves if attacked.

communist

a form of government where all the land, houses, and businesses belong to the government or community

ALLIES

    U.S. allies included the United Kingdom, Canada, and France. These countries and others were part of the North Atlantic Treaty Organization (NATO). Because most were in Western Europe, this side was called the West.

    Soviet allies included Poland, East Germany, and Czechoslovakia. These Eastern European countries were joined by an agreement called the Warsaw Pact. They were known as the East.

> During the Cold War, Germany was split into East Germany and West Germany. The Berlin Wall divided the capital city of Berlin into Eastern and Western sections.

THE NEED FOR SPIES

After World War II, communication and travel between the East and West stopped. Spies who could secretly collect and share information became even more important.

Both the United States and the Soviet Union had spy agencies. The Central Intelligence Agency (CIA) gathered information in foreign countries for the U.S. government. The Soviet Union's spy agency was the KGB.

Other countries had intelligence agencies too. Great Britain's MI6 gathered intelligence on other countries, while MI5 collected information inside Britain. East Germany had a secret police force called Stasi.

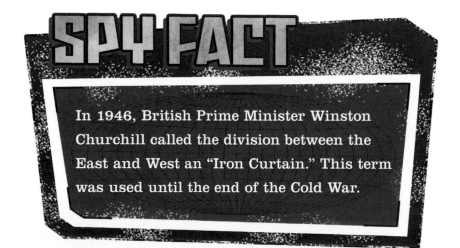

SPY FACT

In 1946, British Prime Minister Winston Churchill called the division between the East and West an "Iron Curtain." This term was used until the end of the Cold War.

CHAPTER 3

THE WEAPONS RACE

LEARN ABOUT:

Nuclear weapons

U-2 crash

Penkovsky and Kennedy

> The United States tested a nuclear bomb
in the South Pacific Ocean in 1946.

The main focus of the Cold War was on weapons. The United States and the Soviet Union pushed to develop bigger and better nuclear bombs. Each country also tried hard to find out what the other was doing.

During the 1940s, the United States developed nuclear weapons at a secret lab in Los Alamos, New Mexico. This program was called the Manhattan Project.

The Soviets learned about the lab. They **recruited** several people who worked there as spies. These people included chemist Harry Gold and scientists Klaus Fuchs and Ted Hall. Other spies were army soldier David Greenglass and engineer Julius Rosenberg. Rosenberg was married to Greenglass' sister, Ethel.

recruit

to ask someone to join a company or organization

SPIES UNMASKED

The United States uncovered the spy ring through a decoding project called Venona. U.S. codebreakers decoded a number of complicated Soviet messages. Only parts of some messages could be decoded. But it was enough information for the United States to realize what was happening.

The Manhattan Project spy scandal shocked and angered Americans. Hall was never charged with a crime, but Fuchs, Gold, and Greenglass went to jail. The Rosenbergs' fate was worse. In 1953, they were put to death in the electric chair.

For the East, the Manhattan Project spy ring was a success. With stolen secrets from the United States, the Soviets finished their first nuclear weapon in 1949. That was at least two years earlier than expected.

> Ethel Rosenberg (left) was executed with her husband, Julius (right). Today, most historians don't believe she was part of the spy ring.

SPYING ON THE SOVIETS

Eastern Europeans caught spying for the West often faced execution. That danger made it hard for the West to recruit Soviet **moles**.

The United States used other methods to learn Soviet secrets. CIA agents searched Soviet news reports. But much of that information wasn't helpful. The Soviet government controlled all newspapers and radio and TV stations.

> The Soviet government controlled its newspapers. *Pravda* (above) was one of the largest.

To understand the Cold War better, imagine two students in a class. Both students are smart, creative, and athletic. They're both leaders. Each has a separate group of friends. These two students are very competitive. One constantly tries to outdo the other. They don't like or trust each other. But each knows the other's strength.

This story helps explain the Cold War. The United States and the Soviet Union are the two students. Allied countries are the friends. Students on each side want to know what the other is doing. They can find out by listening in on conversations. They can dig through desks and lockers. Students can even persuade kids from the other side to share information. But what do you think would happen to students caught "spying" in this manner?

The U.S. military used submarines to search for Soviet communication cables on the ocean floor. When the subs found the cables, scuba divers tapped into the wires. U.S. agents then listened to the messages.

mole

a spy who works within the government of a country in order to supply secret information to another country

THE U-2 AFFAIR

The United States also used spy planes to take photos and gather information from the air. If the plane wasn't seen, the mission worked well. If it was spotted, there were problems.

On May 1, 1960, a U-2 spy plane was flying in Soviet airspace. The Soviets shot down the plane. The pilot, Francis Gary Powers, survived the crash. Soviet soldiers captured and arrested Powers.

The U.S. government said the U-2 was gathering weather information. But the Soviets knew the plane was on a spy mission. Powers was sentenced to 10 years in prison. After two years, the Soviets swapped him for Soviet spy Rudolph Abel. Abel had been arrested in New York City in 1957.

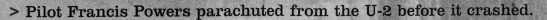
> Pilot Francis Powers parachuted from the U-2 before it crashed.

> Powers held a model of the U-2 plane when he spoke to the U.S. Senate in March 1962.

"SLEEPING" SPIES

A sleeper is a spy who is sent to another country to live a normal life. Sleepers get jobs, become involved in the community, and even raise families. Often, their jobs give them access to valuable information. After months or years, the spy agency contacts the sleeper. The sleeper then becomes an active spy.

One of the most famous Cold War sleepers was Gunter Guillaume. Guillaume moved to West Germany from East Germany in 1956. He later became an assistant to West German Chancellor Willy Brandt. Guillaume used his job to pass secret information to East Germany and the Soviet Union.

In 1974, Guillaume was arrested. Brandt was so embarrassed that he resigned.

> Gunter Guillaume (left) was a trusted assistant to West German leader Willy Brandt (right).

CUBAN MISSILE CRISIS

Sometimes, spies actually helped keep peace during the Cold War. That fact was certainly true in 1962, when the Soviet Union placed its missiles in Cuba. A former Soviet military officer named Oleg Penkovsky worked for the CIA. Penkovsky provided detailed intelligence about the missiles. President Kennedy learned the danger wasn't immediate. Not all of the missiles could be set up and launched right away.

Without this information, Kennedy might have decided to invade Cuba. Then the Soviets would probably have launched nuclear missiles from the Soviet Union. Such an attack could have started another world war.

But Penkovsky's information helped Kennedy remain patient. Kennedy sent American military ships to the waters surrounding Cuba. The ships formed a blockade that prevented Soviet ships from delivering more missiles.

Finally, Kennedy and Soviet Premier Nikita Khrushchev resolved the standoff. Kennedy agreed to remove U.S. missiles from Turkey, which bordered the Soviet Union. In return, Khrushchev removed the Soviet missiles from Cuba.

> Once the Soviets realized that Oleg Penkovsky (center) helped the United States, they arrested and later executed him.

THE END OF THE COLD WAR

> SDI included a sensor in space that would track objects approaching Earth.

Both the United States and the Soviet Union developed powerful weapons. But sometimes, the greatest power of these weapons was the fear they caused.

In the early 1980s, the U.S. government developed the Strategic Defense Initiative (SDI). The SDI was a space system designed to protect the United States from missile attacks. People called it "Star Wars." The SDI used **lasers** and weapons similar to those in the movie *Star Wars*.

At the time, some people said that SDI wasn't practical. The technology wasn't proven to work. Later, tests showed that SDI might not have stopped missiles.

The Star Wars program might not have done what it was designed to do. Still, it was useful. The Soviets were concerned about SDI. That concern led them to spend huge amounts of money on their own military and weapons.

laser

a thin, intense, high-energy beam of light

DISINFORMATION

Spies don't always work to find facts.
They also use disinformation. By spreading
false or unproven information, spies can
damage and confuse enemies. Sometimes
government leaders give untrue information
to reporters. The false information then
ends up in news reports. Other times,
disinformation involves spreading rumors.

In the 1960s, KGB agents created fake
letters that appeared to come from U.S.
officials. The letters were filled with false
information about several African nations.
The KGB sent the letters to African
representatives at the United Nations. The
KGB's goal was to get the Africans angry
with the Americans. Then the Africans
would be more likely to support the Soviets.

The KGB's mail campaign didn't have
much success. But even when disinformation
doesn't work, it can keep people from
thinking about larger issues. Sometimes,
that's enough.

Double agents are similar to moles. They work for one spy agency, but are actually loyal to another. The Cold War had some of the most famous double agents in history.

The Soviet Union recruited Englishman Harold "Kim" Philby as a spy in the 1930s. At the time, Philby was a student at Cambridge University. In 1940, the British intelligence service MI6 hired Philby to spy on the Soviets. The British didn't know that Philby already worked as a Soviet spy.

Philby went to work in Washington, D.C., in 1949. He gathered information on both the British and U.S. governments for the Soviets. By 1963, Philby's British bosses knew he was a double agent. They offered him a deal in exchange for information about the KGB. Philby agreed, but a few days later, he escaped to the Soviet Union.

THE COLD WAR ENDS

By the mid-1980s, it was clear that the Soviet Union couldn't afford to continue the Cold War. Years of huge military spending had left the Soviet government nearly broke. Plus, the Soviets didn't want to fight a nuclear war any more than the Americans did.

Soviet leader Mikhail Gorbachev and U.S. President Ronald Reagan agreed to produce fewer weapons. The next U.S. president, George H. W. Bush, continued building a better relationship between the two countries.

On December 25, 1991, Gorbachev stepped down as Soviet president. One day later, the communist country broke apart. Russia and the smaller countries that made up the Soviet Union became independent. After nearly 50 years, the Cold War was over.

Spying didn't end the Cold War. But it did help keep it from becoming a military war. Spies gave Eastern and Western leaders much information about the other side. This information helped the leaders make decisions that prevented dangerous attacks.

Nobody wanted to start a nuclear war. But without good information, nuclear missiles could have been launched. In that way, spying may have saved millions of lives in both countries.

> Mikhail Gorbachev (left) and Ronald Reagan (right) worked together to end the Cold War.

GLOSSARY

communist (KAHM-yuh-nist) — a form of government where all the land, houses, and businesses belong to the government or community

disinformation (dis-in-for-MAY-shun) — false information that is purposely spread to damage a country or person

double agent (DUH-buhl AY-juhnt) — a person who pretends to be spying for one country, but really is supplying secret information to another country

intelligence (in-TEH-luh-juhnss) — sensitive information collected or analyzed by spies

laser (LAY-zur) — a thin, intense, high-energy beam of light

mole (MOHL) — a spy who works within the government of a country in order to supply secret information to another country

nuclear missile (NOO-klee-ur MISS-uhl) — a powerful explosive weapon that can fly long distances

recruit (ri-KROOT) — to ask someone to join a company or organization

READ MORE

Bjornlund, Britta. *The Cold War.* People at the Center of. San Diego: Blackbirch Press, 2004.

Burnett, Betty. *The Trial of Julius and Ethel Rosenberg: A Primary Source Account.* Great Trials of the 20th Century. New York: Rosen, 2004.

Price, Sean. *Top Secret: Spy Equipment and the Cold War.* American History Through Primary Sources. Chicago: Raintree, 2007.

Sherman, Josepha. *The Cold War.* Chronicle of America's Wars. Minneapolis: Lerner, 2004.

INTERNET SITES

FactHound offers a safe, fun way to find Internet sites related to this book. All of the sites on FactHound have been researched by our staff.

Here's how:
1. Visit *www.facthound.com*
2. Choose your grade level.
3. Type in this book ID **142961305X** for age-appropriate sites. You may also browse subjects by clicking on letters, or by clicking on pictures and words.
4. Click on the **Fetch It** button.

FactHound will fetch the best sites for you!

INDEX